The

Pathway

to

Financial Stability

GOD'S SIMPLE PLAN FOR YOUR FINANCES

Allen Domelle

Visit our website at:
Oldpathsjournal.com
For more copies write:
Allen Domelle Ministries
PO Box 5653
Longview, TX 75608
903.746.9632

TABLE OF CONTENTS

DEDICATION

In July of 2017, I had the privilege of preaching for my good friend, Pastor Rick Walter. During that week of meetings, I taught a lesson on finances during the Sunday school hour. After teaching the lesson, Bro. Walter asked me if I had a recording of the lesson. To my dismay, I didn't have a recording of it, and I couldn't find anyone who did. He told me if I could ever get a recording of what I taught that he would like for me to send it to him because it was so helpful to his people.

After leaving the meeting, the LORD began to work on my heart about the need for a practical book to show Believers how to become financially stable from a scriptural viewpoint. Bro. Walter's prompting led to the writing of this book. Because of Bro. Walter's insight as to the need of this topic, I am dedicating this book to his memory.

There is a reason I'm dedicating it to his memory. The week while I preached for him, he was notified by his doctors that he had cancer. On November 17, 2017, Pastor Walter met his Saviour face-to-face and was forever healed of the cancer he fought for a few short few months.

Pastor Walter was every bit of what a Pastor, husband, father, and friend should be. When you talk to those who were under his ministry, each one talked about how he was there for them in their time of need. Pastor Walter was a faithful husband to his wife, Jennie, and a great father to his children.

As a friend, I can personally attest that he will be greatly missed. I enjoyed the times of fellowship that we had together talking about the ministry and the need for men to stand for the old paths. Bro. Walter never compromised, and to the day of his death stood strongly for the old paths.

It is only fitting that this book is dedicated to Pastor Walter because he was the epitome of stability; which is the key to financial success. As you read the pages of this book, you will benefit from the request of this dear man to get him the recording of my lesson on finances. Though he will never be able to read the pages of this book, his influence to write it will help everyone who reads and follows its advice to benefit through a life of financial stability.

I will be forever grateful to my friend and co-laborer, Pastor Rick Walter, for his part in encouraging me to put the information in this book together.

CHAPTER 1

A CREDIT WORTHY NAME

When I was a young man and starting off in life, I found that it was very hard to borrow money because I had no credit. Many times I found myself almost getting to the point of despair because there was no way that I could establish the credit needed in order to get the loans I needed to purchase cars and eventually a home. Getting yourself to the place where a bank considers you a good risk for a loan is no easy task.

What I have learned since I was a young man is that building credit and keeping your credit good both take the same type of effort. The bank always looks at three things to determine whether you're a good risk. First, they look at your gross income for the year. On any application, they ask you to state your gross income, and they'll also ask you to provide supporting documentation.

After asking about your income, they will ask you about your current debt. They want to make sure you're not over your head with debt before they loan you money. They need to know that your current debts don't cause too big of a risk to loan you money.

The third thing they look at is your past payment history. They want to see, especially within the past few years, that you pay your debts on time. Your past payment history is often a combination of three types of credit. The first type of credit is installment credit. Installment credit requires you to pay a fixed amount based on the amount you borrowed and the time period to which you agreed. This is often a mortgage or car payment. The second type of credit is revolving credit. The amount paid each month is different because it depends on how much credit is used. There is always a minimum payment you will have to pay on revolving credit based on the balance you owe. Credit cards are the most common type of revolving credit. The third type of credit is open credit. Open credit has to be paid in full each month. The most common type of open credit is your utility bill. Open credit is the least likely to impact your credit score, but they may report to the credit bureaus, and if you are late on payments it will adversely affect your score. These three areas combined is what determines your credit score.

The banks combine your credit history on past and existing loans, the amount of debt you have, and your income to determine if you are a good risk to loan money. They want to make sure that you will pay them back on time. They want to be sure that they will get their money back. It is imperative that you pay your bills on time and keep your debt low so that your credit score will stay in the range that allows the banks to see you are qualified to obtain a loan.

The one thing that you always have to understand about banks and money is that banks always look at the risk before they loan money. The interest rate is determined by how big of a risk you are, and if a bank feels that you are going to be a greater risk of possibly not paying their money back, they will charge a higher interest rate. But, if the bank feels that you are a good risk, they will lower the interest rate because they are more confident that they will get their money back.

If your payment history is excellent and you have a steady income, the decision ultimately comes down to your debt to income ratio. They want to make sure that your current debt is not so high that you will not be able to pay back the loan you are seeking. The window that is desirable is normally a 15 percent debt to income ratio, but you really don't want to go any higher than a 25 percent debt to income ratio. They want to make sure you have money left over to pay even if there's a rainy day.

The Scripture says in Proverbs 22:1, *"A good name is rather to be chosen than great riches, and loving favour rather than silver and gold."* You have one chance to make a good name. A credit worthy name is what every Christian should desire to have.

Every Christian should be a good risk for the bank to loan money. Always understand that the bank is loaning you their money. They don't print money, but they're in the business of making money. Therefore, they're going to make sure that whomever they loan money to will pay it back because they're in business to make money. Christian, your desire should be to have such a credit worthy name that when a bank looks at you, they know that you pay your debts.

You have one chance to make a good name. When you ruin that name, it takes several years to rebuild it. Please understand this; you may be reading this book and saying to yourself, "I've got bad credit, and there's no way I can ever rebuild it." May I tell you this, you can always rebuild your name. It may take hard work, sacrifice, and a lot of years to clean up the bad name, but you can always rebuild your way back to a credit worthy name.

If you are ever going to get a loan, you've got to have a good name. God says a good name is better than riches, silver and gold. If at the end of life you don't have all the fancies and possessions that life can give, but you have a good name, you will have succeeded in pleasing the LORD with your money.

CHAPTER 2

THE VALUE OF MONEY

I don't know if you have noticed, but there are no money trees growing money so that we can just go get as much money as we would like. We would love to think that money grows on trees so that any time we needed it, we could go to the tree to get the amount of money that we need, but that is only living in a fantasy world. Money simply does not grow on trees.

Just like everything in life, money is not free. We often say that salvation is free, and it is free for us; however, Jesus still had to pay the price for the gift of salvation so that he could offer it to us for free. Romans 6:23 says, *"For the wages of sin is death; but the gift of God is eternal life through Jesus Christ our Lord."* You will notice the gift is free, but there still is a wage that Jesus paid before He could give us salvation.

2 Thessalonians 3:10 says, *"For even when we were with you, this we commanded you, that if any would not work, neither should he eat."* God is teaching in this verse the principle that money is not free. God is saying that a person should work in order to receive the blessings of obtaining money.

You have to somehow pay for money. When you work a job, you are paying for money. When you get a loan, you are paying for money. Anytime you do an extra task to receive money, that task becomes the payment for money. You will never learn the value of money until you learn that money is not free.

The Scriptures show the principle that money isn't free. Jeremiah 22:13 says, *"Woe unto him that buildeth his house by unrighteousness, and his chambers by wrong; that useth his neighbour's service without wages, and giveth him not for his work;"* You will notice that the laborer was to receive wages for his work. In other words, when you are working on the job, you are buying money with your time. You cannot ignore the principle that money is not free.

In the Scriptures, there was a man who had the mentality that money was free. You find in the story of Matthew 25; a man gave talents to each of his servants to invest so that at his return he could have more money. One of the servants took his talent and buried the money in the ground. When his master returned and demanded what they did with the money, two of the servants doubled their money through investing, but the one servant only had the one talent to give back to his master. This servant was called a *"wicked and slothful servant"* because of his unwillingness to work for money.

The servant with one talent most likely thought that his master would give him another talent when he got back because he didn't "risk" investing his money. The problem with this servant was that he had the mentality that money was free. Money is never free! Just like his master had to work to buy his money, this servant should have worked to buy more money for his master. You cannot separate the fact that any time you receive money, even if it is a gift, that somebody had to work for it. Somebody had to buy that money with their toil, or through investing, so that they could receive more money for their investments.

One of the reasons that so many people get themselves into financial trouble is because they've never learned the principle that money is not free. When you learn that you have to work to get money, you will begin to value every dollar bill that you get instead of squandering it every time it gets into your hands.

One of the greatest lessons that parents should teach their children is that they must work to get money. Until you learn the concept that money is not free, you will waste it, spend it frivolously, and you will never learn the principle of saving money.

When a person learns that money is not free, they start treating money as a valuable commodity. You will see that those who understand that money isn't free will be careful with every dollar they earn, they are frugal in their spending, they will pick up every penny they see, and they will work hard to improve their skills so they can demand more money for their services. Learning the principle that money isn't free will truly change your whole mindset of how you approach your finances.

One of the greatest principles you can learn and teach is that money is not free; therefore, use it wisely so that you have money to pay bills, save for retirement, give, and enjoy life the way that God intended for you to enjoy it.

CHAPTER 3

A Good Name

We live in times when paying debts on time is much easier than it has ever been. Electronic payment plans are set up according to your pay schedule which makes it much easier to pay your debts on time. Banks even allow you to pick the date you want to pay your bill so that you can be sure to be on time with every payment. The Scripture says in Proverbs 22:1, "*A good name is rather to be chosen than great riches, and loving favour rather than silver and gold.*" As I have previously said, it is impossible to keep a good name when you don't pay your bills because a good name is synonymous with paying your debts on time. There are three verses which show us what God thinks about paying our debts on time.

He says in Proverbs 22:1, "*A good name is rather to be chosen than great riches, and loving favour rather than silver and gold.*" God is saying having a good name is better than having all the silver and gold one could desire. If you have silver and gold, but you don't have a good name because you don't pay your debts, the silver and gold don't mean much.

Ecclesiastics 5:5 says, *"Better is it that thou shouldest not vow, than that thou shouldest vow and not pay."* God is teaching that you are better never to make a promise than to promise and not keep it. To make a promise to pay on a certain date and then not follow through with your promise is contradictory to what the LORD wants you to do.

God says in Leviticus 19:11 says, *"Ye shall not steal, neither deal falsely, neither lie one to another."* To make a promise to pay a debt and not pay it is nothing short of lying and stealing from those whom you borrowed money from.

Our goal is to make sure that our name is good, not just as an individual, but also as a Christian. God says it is better not to make a vow than to make a vow and not pay it. In other words, for you to promise to pay your debt on a certain day and not pay it is dealing falsely. You're being dishonest because you promised you would pay by an agreed time.

You may say, "But Bro. Domelle, we have a grace period." Grace periods are for those who have broken the vow of their word. Let me explain. Grace can only be applied when a law is broken. If you don't break a law, you don't need grace. Therefore, grace can only be given after a law, which is the date you promised to make your payment, is broken. When you put your name on the line, or when you swiped your credit card, you promised that you were going to pay by the agreed day. You should never let your grace period be an excuse to be dishonest about paying your debts.

Leviticus 19:11 is literally saying that when you don't pay your debt, you are stealing from that person or institution. You promised that you would pay back their money, and not doing so is stealing from them.

Let me take this one step further. When God says not to deal falsely, He is saying that when you buy something and you know that you don't have the money to pay it back that you are dealing falsely. My friend, by not paying your debts, you are stealing and lying to those from whom you borrowed money, and lying is an abomination to God.

A good name is paying your debts on time. On time means on the day that you promised you would pay it. If you want to be a good Christian, and if you want to please the LORD, you should honor your word. God is a God of truth, and He despises lying. Satan is the father of lies; so when you choose not to pay your debts on time or don't pay them at all, you are doing the work of Satan and not the work of God.

Let me encourage you to re-evaluate how you pay your debts. Always understand this, you can always go to the bank and say you need to readjust your payment date to a certain time, but when you give them that date, you better be sure that you have the money to pay the debt. Paying your debts on time is as important to God as reading the Scriptures daily, being a soul winner, and doing what's right all the time. You should endeavor to be a Christian who has a good name, and you will acquire a good name by always paying your debts when they are due.

CHAPTER 4

OBLIGATIONS BEFORE WANTS

An important principle that everyone must learn at some point in their life is that obligations come before wants. We live in a generation that wants to have everything right now and forgets about the obligations they owe. If we are going to please the LORD, we are going to have to understand the important principle that obligations always come before wants.

Proverbs 22:2 says, *"The rich and poor meet together: the LORD is the maker of them all."* When God says that the rich and poor meet together, He is showing the importance, or teaching that it doesn't matter whether you're rich or poor, the LORD is the priority. In other words, God was showing the importance of keeping the proper order of obligations before wants.

God has a divine order for everything. God teaches the important principle that obligations come before wants in 2 Thessalonians 3:10 when He says, *"For even when we were with you, this we commanded you, that if any would not work, neither should he eat."*

I believe it is very important that everybody understands that God's principle is: work comes before play. When I was a boy, my parents always made me do my chores before I could go out to play. The reason they did this was because they were teaching me God's order was work before play.

Likewise, God's principle is obligations before wants. God's order is to pay your bills before you enjoy the luxuries of life. We live in times when many young people want to have the same pleasures that mom and dad enjoy without first taking care of their financial obligations. What many don't take into consideration is that their parents worked many years to get to the point where they could enjoy the luxuries of a nice home and fancier cars.

A young newly married couple doesn't need to jump into debt trying to get all the fancy cars and luxurious homes that mom and dad have. Instead, they need to learn to work their way through life and take care of their financial obligations before they start fulfilling their wants.

When you have bills to pay, you are obligated to take care of them before you spend money on your wants. Just because you have money in the bank doesn't mean that you have a right to spend that money. Just because you have money doesn't mean that you truly have money. You have bills at the end of the month that will come due, and you must save whatever amount necessary to pay for those bills. You can't go through life thinking that you can make up money at the end of the month when there's no money coming in. I often tell people, when you spend money for bills on going out to eat, you're not right with the LORD. To spend money on luxuries before you pay your bills is wrong. That's why I believe everybody ought to teach their children the importance of working before playing.

When I was a boy, my parents always taught me the importance of caring for my financial obligations before spending my money on wants. At an early age, they taught this to me through the tithe. Whenever I got money, they always made sure that I set ten percent aside for the LORD, because tithing is an obligation. Later, in my teenage years, they taught me the importance of making sure that I pay my bills before spending money on clothing and desires.

Many people today are putting the cart before the horse. They purchase all their wants, and then they don't have money to take care of their financial obligations. As a Christian, God makes it very clear that obligations come before wants. You should always pay your bills before you go out and purchase clothes or spend money on technology that you don't need. You should always pay your bills before you go out to eat or buy the extra things and desires that you want.

In other words, if you're going to please the LORD, and if you're going to be financially stable, you've always got to keep the principle that obligations come before wants. You will find that at the end of life you will have the money to get the things you want if you learn to take care of your financial obligations before your wants. However, if you disregard this principle and spend money on wants before paying your financial obligations, you will find at the end of life you will not have all the desires and luxuries that you want. If you ignore this principle, your obligations will continue to pile up until you have debt that is constantly nagging at you that you will never be able to pay off. Let me encourage you when it comes to your monthly expenses to always remember that you must pay your bills first before you spend any money on wants and luxuries.

Let me also encourage you that just because you have extra money before the end of the month doesn't mean that you should spend it. You should always look ahead and find out if you have bills coming due. Learning this principle that obligations come before wants will help you to become that money-savvy Christian who takes care of the resources that God has given to you. When God sees that you're applying His principle of obligations before wants, you will find that God will tend to bless your finances because He can trust you with His money.

CHAPTER 5

FORESEE EVIL

Life is a series of ups and downs. If you were to look at the stock market and its history, you would find that it has risen and fallen over the years. There is never a time when it always stays up. The stock market always has its corrections when it takes its dips. It is the law of physics that everything that goes up must come down. You cannot expect everything to always be good because there are going to be bad times.

In a normal year, there are four seasons. You have the heat of summer, but you also have the cold of winter. You have a cool of fall, but you also enjoy the warmth of spring. Everything has its ups and downs; everything has its seasons.

Even in the financial world, you have to plan according to financial seasons. The premise that you will always have good times is a false premise. Every day is not going to be a good day financially; likewise, every day is not going to be a bad day. What you must do is foresee your expenses and plan accordingly.

Proverbs 22:3 says, *"A prudent man foreseeth the evil, and hideth himself: but the simple pass on, and are punished."* If you look ahead at what you owe, you can plan your life according to your needs. You must learn that when you have extra money come in you should treat it according to those times when your finances are tight.

I often tell my wife when our finances are tight that it's time to tighten the belt. When I say tighten the belt, you have to understand that my wife knows that I'm not one who likes to spend money. I'm a person who is very frugal in my spending. However, I can foresee that expenses are coming and that I need to save for them now in order to be able to make sure that I have the finances to pay my bills in the lean financial seasons.

As an evangelist, there's always been one season of the year that I've known to be a tight financial season. It is between Thanksgiving and Christmas that I find myself always not having the income that I had the other eleven months of the year. So, what I do is I save the other eleven months so that when those days come, I have the money to make it through those lean weeks.

I often tell people that they need to work their finances off what I call, "Zero balance banking." What I mean by the zero balance banking is this; setting aside a certain amount of money to help you live when finances are tight. When you run your finances off an actual $0 balance in your checking account, you're already in great trouble. I have a set amount that I set aside in my zero balance banking, and when I get close to that number, I tell my wife to tighten the belt and to stop spending as much because we're getting close to that number. If I say that I don't have money, I am saying that I am approaching my zero balance number in my bank account. The zero balance that I use is an amount that I can live on for a couple of months if I lost all sources of income. I would still be able to pay all my monthly bills, mortgage payment, and purchase groceries for a couple of months if all sources of finances dried up. I can make it because of my zero balance banking.

You're going to have to learn to set aside for rainy days. You've got to foresee those expenses just like the Scripture says. You've got to foresee the evil that's coming and hide yourself by having a balance to live on in the financial rainy days. How do you hide yourself financially? You hide yourself by having a cushion of money that you can fall back on in those rainy days. If you don't learn to save money, you will never be able to build that rainy day fund or have zero balance banking to make it in the hard times. It's not going to be easy to get there. But you're going to have to learn not to spend a lot of money and continually set money aside until you get to that point where you have built up your zero balance.

You will find that when you start getting to the point in your financial world where you have extra money set aside for those rainy days, the pressure in life that comes from finances won't be as great as if you didn't have any money. Those who live off a strict zero balance in their checking account are people who are living on the edge and will eventually drift off into financial disaster because they have no money to pay their bills. However, those who learn to save, and those who learn how to have a rainy day fund or zero balance account will be able to make it through those dips in the financial life successfully. One of the reasons God allows you to have good seasons financially is so that you can prepare for the bad seasons.

Let me encourage you to do two things. First, let me encourage you to set a goal of saving a set amount of money aside that you can live on if your financial world collapsed. Second, let me encourage you to stop spending everything you earn. Learn to build your rainy day fund over several months, and you'll be forever thankful in the long run, and your spouse and family will appreciate your financial savvy to be able to anticipate life by caring for them financially when the evil comes.

Certainly, we never know what tomorrow holds; therefore, you better learn to save extra money today. When the evil comes, you will be thankful that you have lived by the zero balance banking concept that I use. That evil could be you not being able to physically work because of health. That evil could be losing a job. That evil could be an unexpected household or vehicle expense. Trust me; you will thank me a thousand times over if you will learn to set aside money that equals two or three months of wages and put it into a savings account for the evil days. Never touch it until the evil day comes. The zero balance fund is for the purpose of tapping into it to make it through the evil days. The pressure of the financial world won't be so great if you learn to foresee expenses and plan accordingly.

CHAPTER 6

LIVING THE SIMPLE LIFE

My grandparents lived most of their lives in a very simple, three-bedroom house in Shelby, Indiana. Saying their house was a three-bedroom house is truly stretching the term three bedrooms. One of the bedrooms was so small that when you got out of bed, you stepped into the living room. The house my grandparents lived in was just a small house where the living room was just big enough to get a couch and one other chair inside of it. The kitchen this house had would be considered very small compared to the homes in which we live today.

My grandparents learned how to live a very simple life. They lived in that little farmhouse for most of their married lives until they moved away to another small house to be closer to their daughter. They lived in the last house until they could no longer live by themselves. The one thing I learned from my grandparents is that you don't have to have a lot of things to be really happy. They learned how to live a simple life, in a simple house, but they were financially stable and happy.

In the latter years of my grandfather's life, my cousin and I managed his finances as we were the executors of his financial world. One thing that became very evident to me as we managed my grandfather's finances was that even though he did not make a lot of money every year, they lived so simply that they were able to enjoy some pleasurable trips in their senior years.

My grandfather worked in the steel mills in the northwestern part of Indiana. He did not make a lot of money. They farmed their land for years and sold the corn to help earn money to pay their bills and set aside for retirement. One thing that was very evident about them was that they didn't spend a lot of money. When my grandfather retired, he and my grandmother were able to purchase a fifth wheel trailer and travel the country and enjoy going to places they always wanted to see. All of this was because they learned how to live the simple life.

I had an uncle who made a statement to me when I was young that influenced my thinking in this area of living a simple life. He said, "Allen, you can have a lot of things when you're young and nothing when you're old; or, you can live a simple life with a few things when you're young, but you will be able to enjoy the things you want when you get old." My grandparents and uncle's advice and lifestyles both had a great impact on my mindset concerning how to live a simple life.

The Scriptures make it very clear that it is better to live humbly than to have possessions and lose your name. Proverbs 22:4 says, *"By humility and the fear of the LORD are riches, and honour, and life."* This verse is teaching the importance of living a humble life; which is a life of living within your financial means. You would be better off if you learned to live a simple life. My friend, you don't have to have a lot of possessions to be happy. Too many people purchase a lot of things when they are young, and the more things they purchase, the more complicated their life becomes. What you don't understand is that you have to pay for those things, and every dollar you spend on those things will truly take away your ability to be able to enjoy the senior years of your life.

I have learned to live simply. I've learned that a $7 watch will tell the time like a $300 watch. I've learned that you don't always have to have the newest technological device that comes out. If you're going to get your finances right and be financially stable in life, you're going to have to understand that you don't need new things every time they come out. It is always better to live the simple life and have fewer things than to have everything. When you fall into the trap of always having to have the newest things that come out, you will find yourself having to deal with financial debt and the pressure that those things place upon your finances.

You will always have to find a way to finance the next new thing if you always have to have the next newest thing. You don't have to have the next newest phone. You don't have to have the nicest shoes. You don't always have to have every accessory that comes with your technology. I'm not saying that you can't enjoy life, but I am saying that it is always better to live a simple life than it is to get your life complicated with a bunch of things with its complicated financing. Debt puts a strain on your finances, and it will cause you to have to figure out ways to make your mortgage payment, car payments, and all the loans that you get including the credit card bills if you continue to add to your debt by wasting money on the newest thing.

My friend, let me encourage you to learn to live the simple life. Let me encourage you to change your mindset from having to get everything that is updated and all the latest gizmos that the stores offer and learn to enjoy what the LORD has given you.

God says in Philippians 4:11, *"Not that I speak in respect of want: for I have learned, in whatsoever state I am, therewith to be content."* God is commanding us to enjoy what we have. When you learn to live the simple life, you will learn that life will be more enjoyable. I tell people often that the richest person is not the person who has the most things or the most money, but the richest person is the person whose wants equal their haves. When your wants and have's equal, you are a rich person. The fastest way to become a rich person is to learn to live the simple life. You will find it much easier to make your wants and haves equal if you live the simple life.

Let me remind you that it is better to live humbly and have a good name than it is to have every newest possession and have a bad name. Life is long, and you will have a chance to enjoy some of the pleasures of life if you learn to live simply when you are younger.

CHAPTER 7

THORNS AND SNARES

If I told you that the next time you go to the store, there would be a thief there to rob you of your money, I would guarantee that you would be sure to keep your money safe. Most likely, you would not even go to that store knowing that someone was going to steal your money.

If I told you that the next time you browse the stores on the internet that somebody was going to steal your financial information, you would not go to those websites. You would do everything you could to avoid the websites where the perpetrator infiltrated, and you would secure your computer to keep your financial information safe.

Most people don't understand that there are many robbers that take your money every day and you don't even realize it. Proverbs 22:5 says, *"Thorns and snares are in the way of the froward: he that doth keep his soul shall be far from them."* The thorns and snares that this verse is talking about are the money robbers that take your money every time you go to the grocery store or browse the internet.

You may say, "Brother Domelle, what robbers are you talking about that steal our money? I don't see any robbers when I go to the grocery store." These robbers that I am talking about are found in the middle of the aisles that have nothing to do with the section in which you are shopping. These robbers are there to grab your attention so that you will purchase that product. That product in the middle of the aisles is what I call a money robber.

Every time you go to the cash register and see all the items that surround the cash register, those are thorns and snares that want to rob you of your money. You didn't go to the store to purchase those items, but they put them there in hopes that they could get more money out of you than you planned on spending.

I love Krispy Kreme donuts. It seems to never fail that when I go to Walmart with my daughter that in the middle of the aisle they'll have Krispy Kreme donuts set up just to lure me. I'm sure they are doing this just to get me to pick up a box and purchase them. As I pass by those donuts, I stop and look, but my daughter says to me, "Dad, you don't need those donuts." I'll continue walking, but those donuts are talking to me. I'll turn my head and begin to walk back, but my daughter grabs my hands and says, "You don't need those donuts." You see, those donuts are a thorn and snare to rob my money. There's nothing wrong with the donuts, but the fact that I didn't go to the store to get them dictates that they are trying to rob me of my money. I went to the store to get another item that I needed, not those donuts.

Whenever you go to the store, you're going to have to learn to have a list of items that you are going to purchase, and then you must determine to stick to that list. You're going to have to learn how to tell yourself, "No."

When you pass by those money robbers that are trying to rob you of your money, you may think to yourself that one dollar here or there is not really going to make or break your finances, but what you don't realize is that one dollar here or there begins to add up. If you spent one dollar a day on thorns and snares, that would be three hundred sixty-five dollars a year that you're spending frivolously. That money could have been used for something else.

Let me try to make this clearer. Just one dollar a day for a whole year will probably equal a car payment. I imagine if I told you that I'm going to give you a car payment so that you only have to make eleven payments a year, you'd be asking what you have to do to get that deal. My answer to you is this; you need to be sure to watch out for the thorns and snares that rob you of your money. You need to be sure that the robbers trying to steal your money through internet advertising don't take your money. You have to learn how to stop looking at all the advertisements. Stop clicking through the advertisements no matter how much they intrigue you.

There are a lot of things that can grab your attention, and these advertisers know it. You have to have the character to say, "No," when those things grab your attention. You may think it is not really that big of an item, but it is taking your money.

Let me encourage you to be careful about the thorns and snares that take the one and two dollars from you. Understand that they are robbing you of your money without a gun. They are stealing your money by placing items in areas of stores where you walk, and on the internet websites that you browse to lure you into listening to your appetite and your desires to purchase something you never planned on purchasing. Thorns and snares will rob you and take money that you could use for bills, investments, retirement, or for your rainy day fund. Beware of the thorns and snares that you see daily and have the strength to deny your desires to accept their lures.

CHAPTER 8

SERVANT OR RULER

Proverbs 22:7 says, *"The rich ruleth over the poor, and the borrower is servant to the lender."* At some point in every person's life they are a servant. What I mean by a servant is that everyone will start out in debt. Most people cannot purchase a house without having debt. A young couple wanting to purchase a home is most likely going to have to get a loan to pay for the house. Most young people don't have the money to purchase a vehicle with cash. So, they have to purchase the car by getting a loan.

Having debt is just a part of life. I know there are some who preach that all debt is bad and that you shouldn't have debt, but I would guarantee you that those who preach such things at some point started out with debt. Any person who has any business sense knows that it takes debt to get started. There would be no businesses if somebody didn't go into debt. Yes, in a fairytale world everyone would have money to go into business without debt. In the make-believe world, young couples would be able to purchase their first home without debt. The problem is, we don't live in a fairytale world; we live in the real world.

A young couple getting started off in their young marriage is going to have to create some debt, which means they are going to be a servant to a lender. Now, there's nothing wrong with being a servant. Although, you'll notice in this verse that God says, *"The rich ruleth over the poor,..."* At some point, you need to move from being a servant to a ruler. At some point in your life you need to have a plan to get yourself out of debt so that you can become the ruler of your finances. Many people never become the ruler because they never control their finances.

The Scripture says, *"But my God shall supply all your need according to his riches in glory by Christ Jesus."* (Philippians 4:19) God always gives us the money to take care of our needs; which means that he also gives us the money to be able to save so we can get out of debt. I believe that one of the greatest mistakes that many believers make is that they continue to put themselves into debt and they're always a servant. Many believers squander the money God supplies on things they don't need, and that is why they will always be a servant.

At some point, you need to have the freedom to be able to say, "Debt does not rule me, but I rule debt." You should have enough assets at some point in your life that you can get out of debt if you sold them. It won't be easy getting there, but with God's help, some planning, and careful control of your finances, you can move from being a servant to the ruler of your finances. Let me encourage you not to fall into the trap of being a servant the rest of your life. Let me encourage you to set up a plan to become a ruler of finances.

One of those ways that you become the ruler in life is that you learn to have as little debt as possible. Be sure that the debt you get into is more of an investment than a debt. What I mean by this statement is that some debt is bad debt because you're immediately losing money when you get the loan, and you will never be able to gain that money back. For instance, a car is a true debt because it depreciates, or loses value. Though you may have to get a loan to purchase the vehicle, you would be wise not to always have to get the most expensive car. If you are wise, you will always purchase a used car. If you get a car that has a few miles or is only one year old, you will be able to take less of a hit on the depreciation.

However, there is some debt that appreciates or gains value, and that debt in itself becomes an investment. For instance, a house is what I would call an investment debt. Yes, you have to go into debt to purchase a house, but if you do your homework, purchasing a house becomes an investment. A house appreciates and gains value over time; before long you will find that, though you may owe on the house, the value of the house is greater than your debt. That, my friend, is an investment debt. Certainly, at some point, you want to be able to pay off your mortgage, but you've now become a ruler of that debt because at any point you need to sell that house you can because the house is more valuable than your debt. When you purchase a house wisely, you will have money to be able to pay off the mortgage; plus, you will have extra money to be able to use for other purposes.

My friend, it is important that every believer becomes a ruler at some point in their life. When you become the ruler of your finances, you will find the pressure of finances will be relieved. When you become the ruler, you will have the freedom to do what the LORD wants you to do without hesitation. When you become the ruler of your finances, you will be able to help more people. When you become the ruler of your finances, you will be able to invest more into the LORD's work. When you become the ruler of your finances, you will be able to enjoy the senior years of your life.

My question to you is this; are you a servant or are you a ruler? Make it your goal to one day become the ruler of your finances if you are a servant. Set up a plan to get yourself out of debt so that you never have to let finances rule you again.

If you are ruler, never leave the status of being a ruler to going back to become a servant. Watch your finances carefully so that you can build your savings. When you build your savings, you can become your own banker and borrow from yourself. When you become your own bank, you then become the ruler of your finances.

CHAPTER 9

IT'S A CHARACTER PROBLEM

I'm always amazed how people tend to attack the tool instead of dealing with the problem. When you attack the tool, you keep the tool from being a benefit to those who it can help. Instead of trying to minimize the usefulness of the tool, you should fix the core of the problem that uses the tool incorrectly.

A mechanic who uses pliers when he should be using a wrench shouldn't throw the pliers away because they can be useful when he has to grip a clamp. Instead of using the tools in a wrong way, the mechanic would be wise to learn how to use his tools properly and also have the character not to abuse them.

It seems in the financial world that it is a common theme to attack the tools of finances. One of those financial tools that is commonly attacked is credit cards. Many financial gurus, who seem to be very interested in charging an exorbitant amount of money to help get you out of debt, will tell you to stop using credit cards. The problem with this mindset is that they're only getting rid of the tool instead of fixing the core of the problem.

The credit card is not the problem. The problem is that an individual doesn't have the character to tell themselves, "No." You can take the credit cards away without fixing the character problem, but you will soon find that same individual will continue to get themselves in a financial mess because they've never fixed their character problem. You'll find those who don't have the character to use their credit cards wisely will also be the same ones who don't have the character to use their cash wisely.

The abuse of credit cards ultimately comes down to poor character and little to no accountability. If every individual corrected their character problem, they would be able to say, "No" to those things that they want to purchase with the credit card. If every individual had financial accountability, they would find that they could use the tool of a credit card for their own benefit.

One fallacy about telling people to get rid of their credit cards is that it takes credit to survive in our present world. I travel just about every week of my life, and without a credit card it would be nearly impossible to reserve a hotel, purchase an airline ticket, or even reserve a rental car when needed.

I know that many do not agree with me on this topic, but I have watched people try to reserve a hotel room with their debit card only to find out that they don't have enough money in their account to hold the room. You may use your debit card to reserve a room, but they are going to hold a set amount of money that may hinder you from being able to use the monies in your account for other necessary items on a trip.

Moreover, reserving a vehicle with a debit card is not as easy as one may think. Consider this; if you use your debit card to reserve a car, what would happen if you were in an accident? What would happen is that your bank account would be locked up and you would have no access to your finances until you can secure money to repay the damages to the rental car company. Not only is this a problem, but many rental car companies will run your credit if you use a debit card. If you have not built credit, this will provide a problem in securing a vehicle for your trip.

I am not saying that you should gather as many credit cards as you can, neither am I saying that you should get as high a credit limit as you can, but I am saying that telling people to survive without a credit card is not sound financial advice. The best advice you can give someone about credit cards is that they need to set up limits and accountabilities with their use of the credit card. Always remember that a credit card is a financial tool that can be used to your benefit. If credit cards are used properly, they can help save you money on vacations or travel.

The problem people get into with their credit cards is truly a covetous problem. The Scriptures are very clear about the sin of covetousness. Jesus said in Luke 12:15, *"...Take heed, and beware of covetousness: for a man's life consisteth not in the abundance of the things which he possesseth."* Covetousness will always cause you to surrender to your desires instead of listening to what is right. When you surrender to your desires thinking that you will be satisfied, you will soon find out that your desires will grow. Ecclesiastes 1:8 says, *"...the eye is not satisfied with seeing..."* The more you feed your covetous appetite, the greater it grows.

The answer to conquering covetousness is found in 1 John 2:15 where it says, *"Love not the world, neither the things that are in the world. If any man love the world, the love of the Father is not in him."* A credit card problem is a love problem. The love of the world and the things of the world will move a person to want more things from the world. Wanting more things from the world will only create debt and poverty.

Like any tool, to keep yourself from abusing its use, you must set up some financial guards. For instance, I often set my car on cruise control to keep myself from speeding. I don't get rid of the car or the accelerator pedal because I go too fast, but I let the cruise control become my safety that keeps me from not paying attention to my speed. The guards you set up will become the cruise control that keeps you from getting into debt.

One way you can keep control of your credit cards is to ask the credit card company to set a lower limit on the amount you can spend in a day. Likewise, you can put a credit limit on your card. If you have a character problem and have difficulties controlling your spending, you would be wise to keep a lower credit limit.

Moreover, if you are trying to correct your credit card spending habits, you would be wise to leave your credit cards at home. Don't make them easily accessible. This will keep you from using them every time you go to the store or restaurant. Learn to create the habit of using cash for most of your spending.

Furthermore, create the habit of paying off your credit card at the end of each month. You are most likely going to use your credit card throughout the month, so at the end of the month pay the complete balance. Paying the balance keeps you from having to pay the high-interest rates that these credit cards charge.

Finally, if you have a severe problem with credit cards, get help from someone who will become your accountability counselor. You are going to have to get someone who can tell you, "No," to whom you will also listen. Having an accountability partner will help you to create a good habit of not running to a credit card for everything you want. Creating good habits with the use of your credit cards is what will keep you from getting into debt.

My friend, credit cards can be great tools, but they can also be great hindrances to your financial future. If you will fix your character problem, you will find that credit card debt won't be a part of your financial future.

CHAPTER 10

A TOOL

I was watching a story on a cable news network about a mother who was upset at the public school where her daughter attended because they allegedly took her daughter's meal away from her. Supposedly, the school didn't care enough for this child to let her eat a decent meal. However, when you heard how the whole incident occurred, you realized that the mother was the one who was at fault.

What happened was the child went through the food line gathering her food to eat, but when the child gave the school personnel her payment card, a card that was supposed to have money put on it by her parents, there was no money on the card. The school policy was that if the child didn't have money, the person in charge of receiving payments was to take the tray of food away and give them a bagged lunch. The bagged lunch was not going to be as good as the warm meal she would get from the buffet bar, but the child was still able to eat. The reporters said that the child was given a cheese sandwich, chips, and something to drink.

The news commentators were livid that a public school would do such a thing to a little child. However, my thoughts were very different from how the story was portrayed about the school. I couldn't believe that a parent would assume that the school should just pay for the child's meal even though it was the parent's responsibility to pay for it.

Our present society has become an entitlement society that believes that everybody else should give us money. What they don't realize is that money is a tool, not a right. Just because you live on this Earth doesn't mean that you are entitled to have money and that people should give it to you whenever you want or need it. Money is a tool. Money is something that you are supposed to earn.

This financial principle reminds me of the parable of talents. The master was about to take a long journey, so he gave each of his servants, three in total, some talents to pay the bills. They were given these to use wisely so that when the master came back, there would be more talents to give back to the master.

One of the servants was not wise with the talent that was given him. His mentality was that money was more of an entitlement. He did not realize that money is a tool that is to be worked in such a manner that you continue to build its value. Instead, this servant took the money that was given him, buried it in the earth, and when his master came back, he gave him the one talent that was given to him.

The master sharply rebuked this servant and said about him, "...Thou wicked and slothful servant, thou knewest that I reap where I sowed not, and gather where I have not strawed: Thou oughtest therefore to have put my money to the exchangers, and then at my coming I should have received mine own with usury." (Matthew 25:26-27) The problem with this servant is that he never learned that money is a tool, not a right.

Jesus said to His disciples in Matthew 10:10, "...the workman is worthy of his meat." Jesus was teaching His disciples that the way you get money is you work for it. You see, money is not a right. Just because others have money doesn't mean that they should give it to you. Money is a tool that is to be earned, and when it is earned, it will be used more wisely.

My advice to every person who is reading this book is to understand that you shouldn't be the type of person who puts your hand out expecting everybody to pay your way. When you start realizing that money is a tool and not a right, you'll be amazed how you will start treating your money differently. You will start becoming the boss of your money instead of spending it frivolously on things that you should not spend it on.

This is why every parent should make sure that their children work for what they get. You should never just give your children money because that is teaching them the wrong mindset. Every parent has a responsibility to train their children that money is a tool that we use to pay our bills and invest so that we can get the most with the money that we have earned.

Everybody is certainly given a different capability with money. Just like in the parable of the talents, one man was given five talents, another man was given two, and the last man was given one talent, but the main difference was the mindset of those three men. Two of them realized that money was a tool, and they used their money as a tool and doubled it. Certainly, there's always going to be some people who have more money than others. That is just life, and we are going to have to accept that not everybody can have the same amount of money.

The main thing we must accept is that money is a tool to finance life, the LORD'S ministry, and to build our retirement. The main thing I want this chapter to do for you is to change your mindset concerning how you look at money. I want you to start realizing that everybody shouldn't be giving you money; they should make you work for it. This is what the Scriptures teach. That is the right thing to do. This is what will help you feel better about yourself at the end of the day when you realize that you have worked for what you have because you understand that money is a tool and not a right.

CHAPTER 11

KNOW THE STATE OF YOUR FLOCKS

Stop reading right now, and write down on a piece of paper the balance in your bank accounts. Once you write down the balances, go check to see if you are close to what you thought you had in the bank. When you are done, come back and finish reading this chapter.

There is an important reason for me asking you to check your current balance in your bank accounts. If you don't know the answer to this question, you are in a very dangerous financial situation. You should always know the balances in your bank accounts. The person who has no idea of how much money they have is the person who is living on the financial edge.

The Scriptures say in Proverbs 27:23, "*Be thou diligent to know the state of thy flocks, and look well to thy herds.*" God is using a shepherd's knowledge of his flock to teach the important principle of always knowing the status of your finances.

One of the responsibilities of the shepherd was to continually count his sheep so he would know if one had strayed, or if maybe a wild animal had taken one of them. Because their wealth was measured by the state, or the amount of their flocks, it was always important to know if all their sheep were in the field. A bad shepherd never kept count of his sheep in the field; whereas, a good shepherd always knew how many sheep he had and where they were. A good shepherd would count to know if one strayed from the flock so that he could recover it.

Let's bring this principle to our finances. If you're going to know the state of your flocks, you need to know how much money you have in your checking and savings account at all times. It is vitally important for the welfare of your finances to know your current balances in each of your accounts. Without knowing these balances, you are literally flying blind and are going to end up crashing financially.

There are some dangers to not knowing the state of your finances. The first danger is that you will never know if you are in financial trouble. How are you going to know how your finances are doing if you don't even know your balances? Too many people just live as if everything is okay, and there is a danger of you acting as if you always know when you don't really know.

The second danger is you will tend to have a false confidence in your finances. That is the biggest problem with many people. Not knowing your balances tends to bring you to a point where you feel there is nothing wrong with your finances which leads to the third danger.

The third danger is that you will tend to spend more freely than if you knew your current financial status. When you don't know where you are financially, you will get a false confidence that gives you mental permission to go ahead and spend money, when in reality, you should be saving money instead of spending it.

However, there are several benefits to knowing the state of your flock. The first benefit is you always know your true financial status. If you ever get around someone who is good with their money, they always know how much money they have. Why? Because they know the state of their flocks. If you want to get control of your finances, you need to know how much money you have in your accounts every day.

The second benefit of knowing the state of your flocks is that it creates a saving mentality. One of the reasons people don't save is because they don't know the state of their financial flock. When you keep a close eye on your finances, you will soon find that you are going to start saving. The shepherd who watched his flock carefully was always careful to make sure that the wolves didn't come in to catch the flock. When you become that shepherd of your finances, you will watch for the wolves that are stealing your money, and you will become a person who saves instead of spending because you will know that you need to build the balance in your accounts.

The third benefit is that you will be more guarded with your spending. If you learn to know the state of your financial flock, you will be a person who guards everything you spend. One of the reasons I am very tight with my spending is because one of my habits every day has been to check the balances in our bank accounts. You will never know your financial status, and you will never become that person who is frugal in spending until you start keeping a close eye on your balances.

The fourth benefit is you will know when to tighten your belt financially. When you are constantly checking your accounts, you will know the real status of your accounts, and there will come a point when, because you are keeping a close eye on your balances, you will have to tighten up your spending so that you can pay your bills.

The fifth benefit is so that you will know how to pray. One of the greatest benefits of being in the know of your account balances is that it enables you to know how to ask God to help you with your finances. Knowing your balances shows you how to be more specific in your prayer life.

What is the balance in your checking account right now? I hope that you know your balances. I'm challenging you to keep a close eye on it every day. You will find when you start keeping an eye on your financial status on a daily basis that your spending and saving habits will greatly benefit.

CHAPTER 12

AUDITING YOURSELF

Every corporation normally has an audit at least once a year. The purpose of this audit is to bring in an outside official to look at their books to be sure that they are spending their money according to the guidelines of their budget. The auditor inspects the accounts to be sure that nobody is taking money away either through embezzling or through frivolous spending. It's all a part of the audit every corporation that wants to keep a good rating for their stockholders will do to be sure they can continue to get people to invest in their company. The audit reveals how well they control their finances.

One of the mistakes that most people make with their finances is that they do not keep good records of their income and spending. I often ask people if they know where all of their money is going, to which they always respond that they do. When they open their accounts and allow me to look at their finances, I begin to figure out how much money they are taking in and where their money is going. It never fails that there is money that is being spent that they didn't realize they were spending.

Being an evangelist has helped me throughout the years to know where my money is being spent. I have to get a receipt for everything that I spend so I can validate my expenditures for my taxes. Those receipts have allowed me to keep a good record of where I'm spending my money, and they also tell me if I'm spending too much money in one area. These receipts reveal if I'm spending money in areas for which I don't have an item in the budget.

Luke Chapter 14:28 says, *"For which of you, intending to build a tower, sitteth not down first, and counteth the cost, whether he have sufficient to finish it?"* This verse is teaching the importance of knowing the whole cost of a project before starting it. You will never know how to set up your budget until you get an idea of where you are spending all of your money.

My advice to you for the next two months is to start getting receipts for everything you purchase. You will never know where your money is being spent until you start getting receipts for your purchases. I don't care if an item costs fifty cents or a hundred dollars, you must get a receipt for everything. Many times we think that a receipt for fifty cents is not needed, but that fifty cents begins to add up and before long it starts creating shortfalls in your budget. You will never be able to get control of your finances until you learn where you are spending your money.

What you need to do is set up a ledger where you can record all of your income. In this ledger, you also need a column named, "Monthly Expenses," and then add a third column and call it, "Actual Expenses." You will find when you build that ledger and start recording your income in the "Income" column that you will have more money coming in than what you initially thought, or you will discover that you have less money coming in than what you originally thought. You must be sure to record every penny that touches your finger on that ledger. If somebody gives you a dollar, record it in the income column of that ledger.

Next, you must list every monthly expense that you think you have in the "Monthly Expenses" column. After you add your expenses in the expense column, start recording your spending in the third column which is the "Actual Expenses" column. The reason you need to get receipts for everything is because the receipts validate what you are putting in the actual expenses column. By the end of two months you are going to find the true story of your finances.

What you have done with this ledger is you have audited your finances. You know where your money is being spent, and at this point, you will also see where to cut your spending to balance your accounts. Getting receipts for everything you purchase and recording those expenditures in the actual expenses column will show you that you are spending money on things that you really don't need.

It is at this point that reality hits you. You will quickly realize that you need to start auditing yourself on a regular basis so that you keep yourself from spending money in areas where you don't need to spend it. You will find yourself in a better financial situation than you were before you started if you audit yourself regularly by keeping records of your income and spending. You will never have a true picture of your financial status until you audit yourself.

CHAPTER 13

YOUR FINANCIAL BOSS

Everybody needs a boss to tell them what to do. A person who never has a boss to tell them what to do is a person who will find themselves in a bad situation in life. The reason many people get themselves into trouble is because they won't listen to their boss when the boss is simply telling them what to do to help them to continue doing what they're supposed to do.

We find in history a people who decided not to have anyone tell them what to do, and that was the children of Israel. In Judges 17:6 it says, *"In those days there was no king in Israel, but every man did that which was right in his own eyes."* These people lived as if they had no boss to tell them what to do; instead, they made themselves their own boss. The problem with this mentality was they found themselves constantly in bondage to the enemy because no one told them what to do and when to do it.

In your finances, you need to have a boss to tell you what to do and when to do it. If you don't have a boss with your finances, you will find yourself in bondage to the enemy of debt. You also find yourself in bondage to the enemy of never having enough money to pay for your expenditures which causes great stress.

The boss in your financial world is your budget. A person without a budget is a person without a boss. Your money will be spent frivolously without a budget, and you will find yourself constantly lacking in your finances. Your budget tells you when to spend your money and where to spend it. It is imperative to have a budget if you want to be financially stable in life. There are seven things you need to consider when setting up a budget.

First, build your budget by your expenses and not your income. In the previous chapter, we talked about the ledger where you recorded your expenses for two months. Those expenses need to be categorized in the budget so you will know where you are spending your money.

Second, determine your income by your net income. In other words, the net income is the actual amount of money you have coming in. When you look at the ledger you created, you will find your actual income in the income column. That is the money that actually touched your fingers. The number in the income column is the number by which you build your budget.

Third, don't forget to put the tithe in your budget. One of the mistakes that many people make is that they put their tithe at the end of the budget when it should be at the top of the budget. The very first thing that comes out of your budget should be ten percent of your income to pay your tithe. You will never be blessed by God if you don't learn to pay your tithes.

Fourth, determine your minimum payments for all expenses. You are going to have to gather your credit card statements and any monthly bills that you have and figure out what the minimum expenses are for each bill. In some cases, you may be stuck with paying the minimum expenses on bills because of your income level. If you don't have enough money to pay extra, you are going to have to pay the minimum.

Fifth, average your changing expenditures by a three-month scale. In other words, your utility bills or other bills sometimes change from month to month. There is no set amount that you can determine for those bills. In this case, add the bills for the last three months, then divide it by three, and that gives you the average of what you are going to spend out every month. The total is the amount that you put in your budget for that item or for that bill.

Sixth, cut out any expenses you don't need. You are going to find when you start building your budget that you may have a shortfall and be in the negative. What you are going to have to do at that point is look at your expenses and find what you can cut out of your life so that you can balance your budget. For instance, if you have cable TV, you may have to cut it out to balance your budget. If you have a phone bill, you may have to go to a cheaper phone plan so you can balance your budget. There are always things in the budget that you can cut out.

May I at this point also suggest that you renegotiate your bills. Don't have the mindset that you have to stay with an insurance company because you have been with them for so many years. Call up other insurance companies and see what kind of price they can get you for comparable insurance. You will often find that when you renegotiate or begin to look for new companies that you can save yourself a lot of money and find money to be able to balance your budget.

Seventh, let your budget tell you where to spend your money. Your budget must now become your boss. If your budget isn't your boss, there is no purpose in setting it up. What you've got to do is look at your budget and determine how much money you have for groceries, utilities, cars payment, dining out, or whatever items you put into your budget. You are going to have to stop spending when there's no money left in that budget item. You must let your budget tell you, "No." You have got to allow your budget to be your boss and tell you that you can't do something if there's no money left in the budget item.

Let me encourage you to take the time to set up a budget. Without a budget, money will leak out of your pockets quicker than you can imagine. When you allow your budget to be your boss, you will find in the long run that you will have more money because you are pulling in the reins of your money, and you will know where your money is being spent. You will also know when you need to cut expenses because they are too high.

Give your finances a boss today. The way you start is by building a budget and letting it become your boss to tell you what you can and cannot do with your money.

CHAPTER 14

Don't Be a Turtle

I often tell people that I hate turtles. It's not that I actually hate a turtle, but I hate the action of turtles when you touch them because they retract back into their shell because they're afraid that they are going to get hurt. I know that this action is God's protective mechanism for the turtle; however, there are inquisitive people like me who would just like to enjoy the turtle but can't because they have retracted into their shell. It is the retraction that causes me to dislike turtles.

So many people are just like a turtle in that they retract into their shell when something comes their way that is uncomfortable. To avoid any confrontation about that area, they go into their little shell and avoid any contact with those who are trying to discuss that area to them. The problem with the turtle mode is that you never give yourself the opportunity to fix your problems.

One of the common habits I find in people who get themselves into financial trouble is that they go into what I call, the turtle mode. The turtle mode is when you are in debt, and you won't read your mail or answer the phone because you know what they are going to say. So, the best way that you know how to handle your situation is to go into your shell and never talk to the creditors and those to whom you owe money. Going into the turtle mode when it comes to your finances only causes your financial problems to compound.

The Scripture says in Proverbs 28:13, *"He that covereth his sins shall not prosper: but whoso confesseth and forsaketh them shall have mercy."* We often tell people that the best way to deal with sin is to face it head on so that you can overcome it. Anyone knows that when it comes to sin, if you hide from the problem of your sin, that it only becomes greater. Sin is just like a cancer; you can pretend that you don't have cancer, but that doesn't take it away.

Likewise, you can pretend that you don't have financial problems, but that doesn't take them away. If you are going to face your problems, you are going to have to get over the turtle mode.

You overcome the turtle mode by first facing the fact that you have a financial problem. You will never get yourself out of debt until you admit that you have debt. You will never be able to catch up on your bills until you admit that you have past due bills that must be paid. Retracting into your little shell doesn't make those bills go away, and it doesn't make your situation get any better.

May I remind you that until you face your problems, your debt is going to keep on getting bigger and bigger. When you let credit card debt go unpaid, the interest continues to compound your debt. When you ignore your debts, they eventually are turned over to the credit bureaus which adversely affects your credit. It will take years to recover from bad credit. If you are going to get out of the turtle mode, you must face your problems.

Moreover, you need to talk to those with whom you have debt. Avoiding those to whom you owe money is not going to make it better. The only way it will get better is when you learn to talk to your creditors. I often tell people that most creditors will work out a solution if you will just talk to them. Your creditors cannot help you if you don't communicate. The biggest thing that you've got to avoid is running away from your creditors.

The best way to deal with your debt is to call those to whom you owe money and tell them about your financial situation to see if you can work out a solution. I promise that you will have a better chance of dealing with your debt by talking to your creditors than you ever will by going into the turtle mode. You must always realize that the creditors just want their money back. This is why they will work with you if you will be honest with them and talk to them about your situation. You will never be able to work out a solution until you come out of your shell and talk.

Never let yourself get into the habit of going into turtle mode when you have to deal with your finances. You must determine that the turtle mode is not for you. Realize that the turtle mode only does one thing; it hurts you. When you start realizing that the turtle mode is more destructive than facing your problems, you will realize that the turtle mode shouldn't be a part of your life. Yes, it is uncomfortable to talk to your creditors about your problems, but it will cause less discomfort than having to deal with greater debt that is caused by slipping into your shell. Decide now to kill your turtle mode and deal with your financial problems. You will never regret getting rid of the shell when you see there is a solution and eventual end to your debt.

CHAPTER 15

COMMUNICATING WITH DEBT

One of the biggest reasons people have problems in life is because they fail to communicate. Anyone who has ever been around me or worked with me knows that I am big on communication. I believe that most breakdowns in any relationship is because of a communication failure. Communication failures often cause misunderstandings with others because they don't have enough information to deal with the present situation.

For instance, many marriages find themselves in trouble because of a communication failure. A husband and wife fail to communicate; thus, they have problems in their marriage. A parent and child often find themselves not getting along with each other because they don't communicate. When a teenager doesn't communicate with their parents, the parents won't understand the teenager which results in a relationship problem.

On the job, it is very important that everyone communicates with each other. The staff needs to communicate with the boss, and the boss needs to communicate with the staff. You will find a lot of strife inside of a workplace that doesn't communicate.

Likewise, when it comes to debt, you have got to learn to communicate with your creditors. When you are in a financial stranglehold and are trying to dig your way out, you cannot do it without communicating with those to whom you owe money. You will never solve your financial problems until you start communicating with your creditors.

Luke 16 tells the story of the unjust steward who had done his boss wrong. He knew that he was in trouble, so he asked himself in verse 3, *"What shall I do?"* He came up with the solution in Luke 16:4 when he said, *"I am resolved what to do, that, when I am put out of the stewardship, they may receive me into their houses."*

The steward planned to go to the people who owed his lord money and offer them a buyout on their debt. For instance, if they owed his boss a hundred measures of oil, he would tell them to write a check for fifty. If a person owed a hundred measures of wheat, he said to write a check for eighty (fourscore). What this unjust steward did was he built a relationship by communicating with those in debt, and worked out a solution for these people to get out of debt. Did the lord get all the money back that they owed? No; but he got money back that he was not going to get if this steward hadn't come up with a payment plan.

You will be surprised how your creditors will work with you if you start communicating with them. However, the first thing you have to do is stop avoiding those to whom you owe money. You must communicate instead of avoiding.

In the previous chapter, we talked about the turtle mode and how we often avoid those to whom we owe money. When getting bills in the mail, the individual in the turtle mode throws the bills away instead of communicating with the creditors. When getting phone calls from creditors, the person in the turtle mode doesn't answer the call because they don't want to talk to them. My friend, this is not going to help you to get out of debt. This is not going to help you to dig your way out of your financial situation. You have got to communicate with your creditors, even when you are going through a rough financial spot in life.

You may not be in debt, but your financial situation may keep you from paying your bills on time. If you will learn not to avoid those to whom you owe money, you would be surprised how they will work with you through your financial hard times.

Let me advise you to swallow your pride and make a call so that you can talk to them about your situation. If you don't make that call, you will always avoid them because you are afraid that they are not going to work with you. You will never know what the creditors are going to do until you make the call. We are so apt to imagine the responses that the creditor is going to say, and then we are surprised once we make the call of how easy they were to work with concerning your situation. The reason they are workable is because they just want to get their money back, and they realize that if you are willing to communicate with them that they have a greater possibility of getting it back. Personally, I am always willing to work with people as long they stay in communication, but once they start avoiding me, that is the very moment that I stop working with them because there is no more communication.

When you make the call to your creditor, you need to be totally transparent about your situation. Nobody can help you if you don't tell them the whole story. If you only tell them part of the story and they later find out that you were not totally transparent, your dishonesty will cause them to distrust you in the future. Be totally transparent about your financial situation and why you are in it. Ask them to help you design a plan to pay them back; but whatever you do, be totally transparent. Don't hide your problems. Don't think that they will never find out. They will find out, and when they find out that you were dishonest with them is when you are going to find that they will stop working with you.

Be totally transparent with the creditor and ask them, "What can I do to make my situation right with you?" You will be surprised how they will begin to talk with you. Yes, some creditors won't work with you, but that is not the norm. You are going to find out that most creditors will work with you in some way. You may still hurt your credit, but working out a plan to pay off your debt is going to make your credit situation a whole lot better in the long run if you follow through with the plan.

Let me challenge you to start down the road of communicating with those to whom you owe money. You will never start down the road to financial recovery until you start communicating with your creditors. You will always find that communication always benefits you in the long run. Don't be afraid to talk to your creditors. Pick up the phone, go to their office, or do whatever you have to do to get in touch with them, and be honest with them so that you can work out a plan to pay them back.

CHAPTER 16

PAY SOMETHING

One mistake many people make when they don't have enough money to pay their bills is that they won't pay the bill at all. The Scriptures are very clear that we are to pay our debts. Romans 13:8 says, *"Owe no man any thing..."* It doesn't matter whether or not we agree with how the creditor deals with our debt, the believer's responsibility is to pay their debt.

God says in Proverbs 22:7, *"The rich ruleth over the poor, and the borrower is servant to the lender."* When you owe someone money, you are their servant. However, there may come a point when you don't have enough money to pay your monthly bill. Let me suggest that instead of not paying your bill at all that you pay something. I believe one of the mistakes we make is that we think because we don't have the money to pay the whole payment that the creditor will not accept any payment at all.

You have got to understand that the creditor needs to see that you are still doing your best to pay your debt. Getting a partial payment is better than not getting any payment at all. Holding the money until you have enough to make the complete payment is just not a wise move to make. Not paying anything on your bill tells the creditor that you are not going to work with them to pay back your debt and that you are likely to default on the money you owe them. This will only make your situation worse.

As we have already talked in previous chapters about the importance of communicating with your creditors, you also must communicate with them when you don't have enough money to make the whole payment. One of the ways that you can communicate with your creditors about your desire to pay your bill is to pay something on your debt. You may not be able to make the whole payment, but can pay something. It may be half of the payment, but at least you are making a payment of some sort to prove you are trying. You are going to find that if you are willing to pay something that it will help the creditor to see that you are at least making an effort at being honest in paying your debts.

Again, making a partial payment will probably damage your credit because you are not making the whole payment, but at least you're making an attempt. As long as they are cashing your checks means that they are willing to take some portion of your payment which will help you in the long run. It is better to do your best than it is to do nothing at all.

The next time you find yourself behind on your bills and you don't have the money to make the whole payment, let me encourage you to call your creditors and ask them if they will accept a portion of your payment and defer the rest of it in another payment.

I believe you'll be pleasantly surprised that creditors understand that people come across hard times, and they will work with you as long as you work with them and are showing them your honesty by communicating and trying to make some sort of payment. Calling your creditors and telling them that you don't have money to pay anything won't help you at all. However, when you call them and tell them that you have enough money to make twenty-five percent or fifty percent of the payment, you'll find that many times they will work with you. You may discover that they will work with you through your situation until you can get back on your feet.

The purpose of paying at least something is to eventually get back to making a whole payment. Don't run from your payments. Don't try to avoid the payments when you get behind. Pay something! Try to defer it until you get caught up with your creditor; this is just being honest. The best thing you can do as a believer of Jesus Christ to keep your testimony is to pay something, because something is better than nothing.

CHAPTER 17

GET A JOB

The key to financial stability is having a source of income to pay your bills. There's only one way to establish income, and that is through working a job. If you are going to get a job so that you can become financially stable, you must never acquire the mindset that you are above any job.

Years ago, I worked in construction. One day a friend of mine came to me and told me that if I ever needed a side job that I could work with him. I asked him what the job was that he was offering. He told me that it was working as a coroner's assistant, which meant my job was to pick up dead bodies. I remember telling him that I would **never** do something like that. Saying, "Never," was the worst thing I could have said. What I didn't realize was three weeks later I would be without a job because our next contract was not ready to be started for at least three to four weeks. I had payments that were coming due, and I needed money to pay those bills. Reluctantly, I called my friend and asked him if the job was still available. He told me that it was, and I found myself picking up dead bodies as a side job. I took the job, not because I wanted to do this type of job, but because I needed money to pay my bills.

It is vitally important that you don't let laziness keep you from working an "unpleasant" job. A lazy person will never be financially stable. A lazy person always lacks in their finances. Proverbs 10:5 says, *"He that gathereth in summer is a wise son: but he that sleepeth in harvest is a son that causeth shame."* You will find that lazy people always have an excuse as to why they can't work, but you will also find that lazy people are not financially stable.

Proverbs 14:23 says, *"In all labour there is profit: but the talk of the lips tendeth only to penury."* You can talk all day about your desire to become financially stable, but you are going to have to get a job to make this happen. If you are going to pay your bills, save money, and eventually have money set aside for those rainy days when something happens, you must be willing to work a job, even if it is unpleasant.

A person without a job needs to have the mindset that their job must be to find a job. Proverbs 12:24 says, *"The hand of the diligent shall bear rule: but the slothful shall be under tribute."* I've always found that those who are diligent and work hard at finding a job always find a job. You must be diligent in your search for a job. The best way to be diligent in your job search is to spend the same amount of time trying to find a job as you would if you worked a regular job. You will never find a job by sitting at home, but you will find a job by diligently searching for a job as if it was your job.

When you get behind financially, you may also need a second job to get yourself back on your feet. Don't be above working more than one job. When you need money to pay your bills, sometimes working two jobs is the only way you can make this happen.

Moreover, don't wait until you are behind to get serious about finding a job. Be aggressive about finding a job as soon as you are unemployed. I often tell people that if you are aggressive about finding a job that you can find one; however, if you wait until your bills pile up to get serious, you will always be playing catch up.

Let me also advise you that if you don't hear back from an employer when you are looking for a job to go to the place of employment and ask them if they have reviewed your application. This shows them how serious you are about working for them. You can tell me all day long that you've put your applications in, but don't let that application sit there. Go back and talk to the employer to see if they are still hiring. This shows them your desire to work for them, and it will also tell you if you need to take them off your list of places for possible employment.

Let me also warn you never to be late to an interview. If you're late to an interview, you are telling the employer that you will always be late to work. No employer wants to hire someone who is undependable when it is time to go to work. Be there on time, and be ready to go to work immediately.

If you're going to be financially stable, you are going to have to have a job. Every person who is financially stable has worked a job, and you are no different. Be careful about getting the mindset that you are above a job. Be willing to work any job as long as it doesn't contradict the Scriptures. Work hard and be dependable. You will find if you work hard that you'll be promoted, which will lead to a raise; thus, giving you more money to help you become financially stable.

CHAPTER 18

Clean House

A story is found in 2 Kings about a widowed lady who got behind on her bills and was about ready to lose her son to the creditors. In those days, if you didn't pay your bills, the creditors took the children and sold them as slaves for payment of debt.

This widow lady was the wife of a prophet, and for whatever reason, this man didn't set money aside for his family if he died. This lady knew her only hope to get out of debt was to go to the man of God.

The Scriptures tell us that she went to Elisha and told him her situation, to which he replied, *"...what hast thou in the house?"* (2 Kings 14:2) This was the key to her getting out of debt. He knew that there had to be something in her house that she could sell to make money. She replied that she only had one pot of oil. Elisha told her to borrow as many pots and pans as she could, bring the pots and pans into her house and pour oil into them. Once she was done pouring the oil, she was to sell it to pay her bills. What this lady found out was that she had the resources all along to pay her bills.

An important principle is being taught in this verse. God is teaching that there is always something you can find in your house that can produce extra money or income to help you become financially stable. We live in a digital age which makes it much easier to sell things to help pay down debt or to increase our income.

If you're going to become financially stable, you need to clean your house and find things that you can sell. You will be amazed that inside of your house are things that you don't use any more that could be sold on a digital platform to make money.

Let me help you out with this project. If you haven't used an item for one year, you don't need it. I know you think that you may use it someday, but if you haven't used it in one year, most likely you are not going to use it in the next year. It is worthless to let things sit around the house and fill up a closet when you could use it to help raise money to pay bills or to put money into savings. Don't become a packrat. Learn to let go and sell things that are in your house.

Let me also warn you not to be tempted to use the proceeds of the sale to waste on personal desires. If you are not careful, you can have a garage sale, or sell things on a digital platform, and be tempted to spend that extra money on something that you want instead of using it for what you originally intended. Don't let the temptation to buy something you want cause you to take the extra money and misappropriate it in the wrong area.

Let me also encourage you to use your talents to make extra money. My wife is a master of using her talents to help people, but there have also been times she's used her talents to sell things for extra money. I've met ladies in churches who are very good at making jelly and turned their talent into a source of income by selling jelly at a farmer's market or online through a digital platform. Whatever your talent is, God gave it to you for a reason; use it to make extra money to help you to become financially stable.

Finally, don't let emotional ties keep you from getting yourself out of debt. When you find things in your house, don't let your emotional ties keep you from using them to earn an income. You must realize that God might have given those things to you to help you in your current situation. Let the unused possessions in your house become the money makers to help you become closer to financial stability.

CHAPTER 19

THE RIGHT MINDSET TOWARDS MONEY

One of the most important things to becoming financially stable is having a proper source mindset concerning money. Proverbs 10:3 says, *"The LORD will not suffer the soul of the righteous to famish: but he casteth away the substance of the wicked."* You must always understand that all of your money belongs to God. A proper source mindset concerning money is simply realizing that you are a steward of God's money and that you must use it according to how He would use it.

A proper source mindset realizes that God gives us money, and He is also the One who has the ability to take it away. Philippians 4:19 says, *"But my God shall supply all your need according to his riches in glory by Christ Jesus."* Never forget that God is the source of all income. This is why it is important that you keep the right mindset about money. When you understand that God is the source of all money, you will begin to realize who your money truly belongs to. When you realize that God is the one Who gives you everything, it is then as the believer that you will go to the LORD and ask Him to supply your needs.

The mistake you must not make is thinking that the money you make is yours. Job 1:21 says, "...*Naked came I out of my mother's womb, and naked shall I return thither: the LORD gave, and the LORD hath taken away; blessed be the name of the LORD.*" One of the things that helped Job get through his hard times is that he completely understood that God was the owner of everything. He understood that God gave him money, and because He gave it to him, He also had the right to take it away.

You are going to have to understand that the money you make is not yours; but it is God's. When you get the right mindset towards your money, it is then that you will realize that you are only a steward of God's money. When you realize this, you will begin to use your money more wisely. Many people spend money frivolously because they think they have a right to because it's their money. When you realize that you are the steward of God's money that He has entrusted to you, you will begin to be extra careful in how you spend it because you realize it belongs to Him. Every penny that you have in your accounts belong to God. Don't ever forget that! When you have a right mindset about who your money belongs to and who gives it to you, you will find your mindset towards how you spend, use, or invest that money will begin to change.

Let me encourage you with your finances to always be careful about using money as if you are the owner. When you have the mindset that your money belongs to God, you will ask Him about whether or not you should spend money on things that you desire. I don't believe that God wants His people to live as paupers their entire life, but I do believe that every believer should ask the LORD whether they should spend His money on the things that they want to purchase.

Think with me about this; imagine when you go to buy a car if you asked the LORD if He would want you to purchase the car. Imagine if you asked the LORD if this is a good investment with His money. I believe you would be more careful about which car you purchased if you did this. I also believe that you wouldn't be purchasing a car that is not really needed.

Imagine asking the LORD before you spend money on items that you personally desire if He would want you to use His money on the item. Do you see where I'm going with this mindset? Do you see how having the right mindset towards your money can help you to be more careful with your spending?

Having a proper source mindset about money will help you to spend it the way that God would spend it if He were in your shoes. Don't let Satan trick you into believing it's your money. Accept the Scriptural mindset that God wants you to have about every penny you earn. Adopt the mindset that all of your money belongs to God and that you must spend it the same way He would if He were in your shoes. This will keep you from spending money on things you really don't need.

CHAPTER 20

A RIGHTEOUS PAYCHECK

If I told you that a certain lifestyle could help you earn thousands of dollars every year, I imagine that you would want to find out what that lifestyle is so you could pursue it. I want to tell you that there is a lifestyle that you can live that will keep you from spending large amounts of money on things that you don't need.

Proverbs 10:2 says, *"Treasures of wickedness profit nothing: but righteousness delivereth from death."* The lifestyle I am talking about that is found in this verse is that righteous living and serving the LORD always saves a lot of money. Have you ever stopped to consider how expensive a sinful lifestyle is? If you looked at the expense of living in sin and compared it to the savings of serving the LORD, you would be highly motivated never to live another day in sin.

Just think about how expensive it is for a person to smoke cigarettes. A pack of cigarettes is very expensive. Let's just say a person smoked one pack of cigarettes a day. If you multiplied the cost of one pack of cigarettes by how many packs they smoke a year, you would find that not smoking is actually a cheaper lifestyle and will give you more money than if you smoked cigarettes.

If a person chooses to drink alcohol, they are wasting money they could better use for many other purposes. If you looked at look at how much it costs to purchase a carton of beer, you would realize that you could save yourself hundreds, if not thousands of dollars every year if you didn't drink beer.

I'm a big believer and proponent that living for the LORD always saves money. Consider the importance of marrying the right person. By marrying the right person or working out your marital issues with your spouse, you can save yourself thousands of dollars throughout the years. Working out marital issues is much cheaper than getting a divorce. Have you considered the expense of child support and alimony? Have you considered what it would cost to go through a divorce and how much extra money you would have the rest of your life if you didn't have to pay alimony or child support because of your divorce? My friend, serving the LORD always produces a less expensive lifestyle.

I'm not saying that people cannot become financially stable who don't live these lifestyles, but I am saying that you can have more money in your checking account a whole lot quicker if you live a righteous life.

God gives the right way to live in His Word, and if you follow His prescription of living, you will find that it is much cheaper than Satan's offer to live in the world. The world will steal your money through its addicting lifestyles. People addicted to drugs spend thousands of dollars trying to fix their habits; however, if you just stayed clean and kept your body from drugs, you wouldn't have to spend thousands of dollars on drugs or drug rehab.

Let me ask you this question; what is in your lifestyle right now that is robbing you of money? What sin could you quit that would save you hundreds, if not thousands of dollars? I encourage you to start living right. Let me point out that you would have much more money if you lived for the LORD. The righteous lifestyle is a paycheck in itself. If you live right, righteousness will pay you back thousands of dollars every year. You say, How do I find money? Get rid of sin, and you will find money that you didn't have before.

CHAPTER 21

A BAG WITH HOLES

Haggai 1:6-7 says, "Ye have sown much, and bring in little; ye eat, but ye have not enough; ye drink, but ye are not filled with drink; ye clothe you, but there is none warm; and he that earneth wages earneth wages to put it into a bag with holes. Thus saith the LORD of hosts; Consider your ways." I'm afraid that many times people find themselves seemingly doing everything right, but never getting ahead. Have you ever been there? Has it ever seemed like you are constantly putting your money into a bag, and when you go to reach into the bag the money is not there? I believe many people have found themselves putting money into a bag with holes that leaks their money into places where they don't even know where it's going.

There is a reason why I've left this chapter to the end. The reason I made this the last chapter is because I wanted you to read the whole book without rolling your eyes about a preacher talking about the importance of paying your tithe. If I were to put these chapters in the order of God's emphasis, this would be first chapter of the book because God cannot and bless your finances without tithing.

Malachi 3:10 says, "Bring ye all the tithes into the storehouse, that there may be meat in mine house, and prove me now herewith, saith the LORD of hosts, if I will not open you the windows of heaven, and pour you out a blessing, that there shall not be room enough to receive it." I'm afraid that many times we don't look at tithing through the eyes of God. A tithe is simply ten percent of your income; likewise, the tithe belongs to God.

As a boy, my parents taught me the importance of giving ten percent of my income to God. If I received money from family or friends for my birthday or Christmas, my parents would remind me that ten percent belonged to God. When I did side jobs as a young boy, they took my money and laid it on the table and reminded me that ten percent of that money belonged to God.

We previously talked about the proper source mindset that your money belongs to God. It is imperative for you to realize that it is very generous of God to only ask for ten percent of His money back and allow you to live on the remaining ninety percent. It would never bother you to pay ten percent of your income to God if you realized that every dime in your bank account belongs to God, and that He is allowing you to use His money to pay your bills. It shouldn't bother anyone to give God ten percent and live on the ninety percent; but sadly, many people have a problem with tithing.

You may think that you can't afford to tithe, but let me emphatically say that you can't afford not to tithe. You must tithe if you want God to bless you and your finances. God says in Malachi 3:8-9, *"Will a man rob God? Yet ye have robbed me. But ye say, Wherein have we robbed thee? In tithes and offerings. Ye are cursed with a curse: for ye have robbed me, even this whole nation."* God makes it very clear that He curses those who don't pay their tithe. If you don't want God to curse your finances, you had better start giving him ten percent of your income.

Malachi 3:11 says, *"And I will rebuke the devourer for your sakes, and he shall not destroy the fruits of your ground; neither shall your vine cast her fruit before the time in the field, saith the LORD of hosts."* God makes it very clear that when you tithe, He protects you and your money; however, when you don't tithe, you are inviting God to take His hand away and to curse your finances.

Maybe you are thinking that you don't know how you can afford to tithe. Let me remind you that you can lways afford to tithe because it is the first bill you pay. ι may not be able to afford going out to eat, but ⌐an always afford to tithe. You may not be able to ⌐he money for snacks, but you can always afford to pay your tithe. You've always got to understand that paying your tithe is the first thing you do with the money you earn. As soon as you get your paycheck, you should take out ten percent to pay your tithe before you start paying your bills.

Maybe you think that you can't afford to pay your tithe. God dares you in Malachi 3:10 to tithe when He says, *"...prove me now herewith, saith the LORD of hosts, if I will not open you the windows of heaven, and pour you out a blessing, that there shall not be room enough to receive it."* God is saying to put Him to the test to see if you can give more than what He gives to you.

2 Corinthians 9:6 says, *"...He which soweth sparingly shall reap also sparingly; and he which soweth bountifully shall reap also bountifully."* My friend, you cannot out-give God. Luke 6:38 says, *"Give, and it shall be given unto you; good measure, pressed down, and shaken together, and running over, shall men give into your bosom. For with the same measure that ye mete withal it shall be measured to you again."*

God promises that if you give Him your tithe that He will bless you. I'm not saying that He's going to make you a millionaire, but I am saying that He will make sure that your needs are met. If you don't want your finances to be cursed, you better be sure to pay God the ten percent that you owe Him.

Let me make it clear that a tithe is just as important as your mortgage payment. Let me say it more emphatically that a tithe is more important than your mortgage payment because if you don't pay your tithe, God will take His protecting hand away from your finances. If you don't want to be putting your money into a bag with holes, you had better be sure to pay your tithe. Certainly, you must pay your mortgage payment, but the bank doesn't pay you back when you make a payment. God makes a great deal with the believer in promising that He will reward them for paying their tithe by giving them more than they paid Him. God challenges you to test Him and see if He won't bless you more.

Everyone who has ever paid tithes has always had money to take care of their financial needs. If you want your finances to be blessed, you had better pay God His ten percent.

I have heard some say that if you can't afford to pay ten percent that you should tithe five percent. My friend, you can't tithe five percent or seven percent because a tithe is ten percent. If you choose to give God five or seven percent, you are still not paying your tithe, and He will judge you for it. Tithing is ·ying ten percent of your income, and nothing less! e you pay ten percent, you have tithed on your ə.

Let me encourage you not to be tempted to take the tithe away from God. Always understand that the first thing you do when you get money is to pay your tithe and plan your budget on the remaining ninety percent. You will always find that God's blessings will be on your finances when you tithe.